HOLY DAY
(THE RED SEA)

Andrew Bovell

Currency Press, Sydney

CURRENCY PLAYS

Holy Day first published in 2001
by Currency Press Pty Ltd,
PO Box 2287, Strawberry Hills, NSW, 2012, Australia
enquiries@currency.com.au
www.currency.com.au

This revised edition published 2004

NATIONAL LIBRARY OF AUSTRALIA CIP DATA
    Bovell, Andrew.
        Holy day (The Red Sea).
        Rev. ed.
        ISBN 0 86819 740 8.
        I. Title.
    A822.3

Set by Dean Nottle
Printed by Southwood Press, Marrickville, NSW

Contents

Holy Day was first produced by State Theatre Company of South Australia at The Playhouse, Adelaide Festival Centre, on 21 August 2001, with the following cast:

EPSTEIN	Peter Docker
WAKEFIELD	Frank Gallacher
CORNELIUS	Cameron Goodall
GOUNDRY	Dino Marnika
LINDA	Rachael Maza
ELIZABETH	Mandy McElhinney
OBEDIENCE	Melodie Reynolds
NORA	Kerry Walker

Director, Rosalba Clemente
Designer, Cath Cantlon
Lighting Designer, Mark Shelton
Composer, Bernie Lynch
Assistant Director, Sam Haren

CHARACTERS

NORA RYAN, 40s, the hostess of the Traveller's Rest
OBEDIENCE RYAN, 17, Nora's daughter
ELIZABETH WILKES, 30s, a missionary's wife
THOMAS WAKEFIELD, 40s, a settler
LINDA, 20s, a traveller
SAMUEL EPSTEIN, 30s, a traveller
NATHANIEL GOUNDRY, 30s, a traveller
EDWARD CORNELIUS, 16, a traveller

SETTING

The white frontier. The mid-nineteenth century.

OPENING

A mission station.

Black clouds loom over a vast desert plain. Lightning cuts the sky on the horizon. Thunder rumbles in the distance.

A woman emerges from the remnant smoke of a fire. Her face is pale. Her hair has fallen. She is bleeding from a cut above her eye. She holds a shawl draped in her open hands. She is praying.

ELIZABETH: Do my justice, Lord, and fight my fight against a faithless people. From the deceitful and impious, rescue me. From the impure, protect me. For You, Lord, are my strength. Why do you keep me so far away? Send forth Your light and Your fidelity. They shall lead me on and bring me to the Holy Day. Then I will go to the altar of God. Then I shall eat of His body and drink of His blood, the blood of my gladness and joy...

A single gunshot is heard. The shawl drops from her hands.

A hundred crows darken the sky, startled by the shot.

ELIZABETH *is still.*

Now it is finished...

She does not move.

The sound of thunder in the distance.

◆ ◆ ◆ ◆ ◆

ACT ONE

SCENE ONE

The Traveller's Rest—a halfway house between distant settlements.
Dusk.

NORA RYAN *is chopping wood. She handles the axe as well as any*
man. We watch the rhythm of her work, the arc of the axe and the
split of the wood. She looks up at the sound of approaching thunder.

OBEDIENCE, *a girl on the cusp of womanhood, comes to the door of*
the Rest. They listen as the thunder roles away to silence.

NORA: Light the lamps, girl… Keep the night away.

> OBEDIENCE *turns back into the Rest.* NORA *gathers her pile*
> *of wood.*

Let the world know we're here… As if the world cares.

> *A woman is standing on the edge of the clearing. We sense*
> *she has been there some time, watching.*

LINDA: Missus…

> NORA *looks up.*

Some work, Missus.

> OBEDIENCE *watches from the door.*

NORA: [*seeing her*] Go inside.

> OBEDIENCE *moves back into the Rest.*

I've got nothing.

LINDA: Some tucker then.

NORA: No.

LINDA: Just some bread, hey?

NORA: I said I've got nothing for you, now clear off.

> *Beat.*

LINDA: Storm's coming, Missus.

> LINDA *moves away into the darkness.* NORA *watches her go.*

◆ ◆ ◆

Inside the Rest.

OBEDIENCE *moves away from the door from where she has been watching. She proceeds to light the lamps. She hums a sweet tune as she works. The glow from the lamps gradually reveals a simple bush cottage, tenuous shelter against harsh surrounds.* OBEDIENCE *becomes quiet as* NORA *enters with her pile of wood and places it by the stove. She stokes the fire as* OBEDIENCE *washes down the table in preparation for the night's custom.*

NORA: Who taught you that tune?

OBEDIENCE: No one.

NORA: Just came into your head, did it?

OBEDIENCE: Must've.

NORA: Those mission blacks been down here?

OBEDIENCE: No.

NORA: You stay away from them.

OBEDIENCE: It's just a song.

NORA: It's a bloody stinking English hymn and I'll not have it sung in my house. [*She stokes the fire and checks a pot on the stove.*] They talk to you much about God?

> OBEDIENCE *shakes her head.*

Good, 'cause God's a big ugly whitefella. He doesn't come round here much 'cause he knows if he does I'll spit in his face and kick him in the arse.

> OBEDIENCE *smiles.*

You think I'm joking.

OBEDIENCE: I heard…

NORA: Here we go…

OBEDIENCE: [*lighting the lamp at the door*] That the sun doesn't shine much in England.

NORA: That's true.

OBEDIENCE: That it rains all the time.

NORA: That's true too. It's a piss awful place. Now Ireland's another matter. The sun always shines in Ireland.

> NORA *laughs at the thought of it.* OBEDIENCE *sees something outside.*

OBEDIENCE: There're travellers coming.

> NORA *moves to the door and looks out.*

NORA: So the night might be worth something after all. Be ready, girl They'll want to eat. [*Leaving*] And keep your tongue to yourself until I get back.

> NORA *moves into the back room.* OBEDIENCE *sets the table with three bowls and a loaf of rough bread.*
>
> *Three travellers enter the Rest*—NATHANIEL GOUNDRY, SAMUEL EPSTEIN *and* EDWARD CORNELIUS. *They lay their swags at the door and take their place at the table as* OBEDIENCE *fills their bowls from the large pot on the stove.*
>
> *A crack of thunder outside.* OBEDIENCE *starts. It quietens. She senses something. She looks to see the youngest of the travellers* EDWARD CORNELIUS, *watching her. She moves away.*
>
> GOUNDRY *breaks the bread into three pieces and passes them to his companions. They eat in silence, driven by the hunger from being on the road.* CORNELIUS *remains aware of* OBEDIENCE *keeping her in the corner of his eye.*

EPSTEIN: Some grog.

OBEDIENCE: [*quietly*] The mistress will come.

EPSTEIN: Speak up.

OBEDIENCE: The mistress has the key.

EPSTEIN: Where is she?

> OBEDIENCE *indicates out the back.*

GOUNDRY: And your master?

> OBEDIENCE *is silent.* GOUNDRY *smiles, knowing now that there is no man here.*
>
> *The wind is building outside. The walls rattle. Hessian billows. A gust takes the flame of the lamp at the door* OBEDIENCE *moves to relight it.*

[*To* CORNELIUS] She's pretty, isn't she?

> CORNELIUS *looks away.*

Got a touch of the chalk in her.

> *As* OBEDIENCE *moves back from the door* GOUNDRY *takes her by the arm.*

You can have her if you want.

> NORA *stands at the door. Her hair has been tied up.*

NORA: Eat your food, gentlemen. It might be your last. The road from here travels forever and you'll soon find yourselves on it if it's trouble you want to cause.

> GOUNDRY *lets* OBEDIENCE *go.*

GOUNDRY: It's not trouble, Missus, just a bit of sport.

NORA: I've seen your kind of sport before.

EPSTEIN: We want some grog.

NORA: Then put your money on the table.

> EPSTEIN *places coins on the table.* NORA *sweeps them into her palm and disappears out the back.*

GOUNDRY: No place for a woman, hey Samuel? Not alone. Least not a white one.

EPSTEIN: Leave it alone, Goundry. I'm too tired for it.

> NORA *enters with a jug of grog and three mugs.*

GOUNDRY: What do you say, hostess? No place for a woman out here.

NORA: [*pouring*] I say the mouths of travellers are best left to eating than to wondering where a woman should or shouldn't be.

EPSTEIN: We're looking for work.

NORA: You won't find it here.

EPSTEIN: We heard there're farms out this way.

NORA: Most have tried and moved on. And taken their business with them. A few are still clearing. They might take you on for food and board.

GOUNDRY: Do you take us for blacks?

NORA: So you think you're worth a wage, do you?

EPSTEIN: An honest wage for honest labour, yes.

NORA: Why would men pay the likes of you when there's blacks that'll do the work for free?

GOUNDRY: There's nothing wrong with the likes of us. [*Beat.*] You want to mind what you say.

NORA: I'll say what I want in my own house, Mister.

EPSTEIN: We heard there'd been trouble with the blacks up here.

NORA: A few sheep speared. No more than that.

GOUNDRY: There's nothing but empty shacks for thirty miles back along that road.

NORA: It's the land that's driven them off, not the blacks. Men from the gutters of London who wouldn't know the difference between a sheep's arse and their wife's arse and wouldn't care if they did.

EPSTEIN: You think a free man has a choice how he makes a living out here.

NORA: Are you free men then?

> EPSTEIN *doesn't reply.*

There's a farmer near here, two miles on, by the name of Wakefield. He likes to think he's a fair man. He might take you on. Now enjoy your drink and you'll sleep well tonight. You're lucky to be in before the storm.

> GOUNDRY *is standing at the door, looking out to the bush.*

GOUNDRY: Two white men speared in the back not twenty miles from here. And a farmer and his wife burned to death in their shack. They say they had the woman before they killed her.

NORA: I've heard the story.

GOUNDRY: How do you sleep at night?

NORA: They don't bother me.

GOUNDRY: Still, I'd not have a blackfella on my land, even if he did work for free. Not when there's white men wanting the jobs.

NORA: Two with tongues that keep wagging and one with the sense to keep his still.

GOUNDRY: His eyes say clearly enough what he wants.

NORA: [*indicating* OBEDIENCE] The hand that touches her is food for my dog.

GOUNDRY: Come on, hostess. Extend your hospitality a little. We'll pay for her.

NORA: She's not for sale.

GOUNDRY: Then we'll take her for free.

NORA: [*to* OBEDIENCE] Out of here.

GOUNDRY: We've come a long way, woman, with nothing but the reputation of this Rest to drive us forward. We're in no mood to be denied.

NORA: If the reputation of my Rest travels far then you would have also heard that many have left it minus the poxy piece of meat that hangs between their legs and makes them a man.

> OBEDIENCE *moves to the door.* GOUNDRY *moves to block her way.*

Leave the girl. She's all bone and wouldn't know what gives a man pleasure. Drink your grog and later, I promise, you'll have what you've travelled so far for. Even your mute companion, though he's far from a girl's dream, will have his fill... that is unless he's lost more than his tongue.

GOUNDRY: He's a dumb bastard but he lacks for nothing where it counts.

NORA: Is that so?

GOUNDRY: [*to* CORNELIUS] Show the hostess what you have. She wants to see if you're worth the trouble.

NORA: [*to* OBEDIENCE] Go.

> OBEDIENCE *exits.* CORNELIUS *doesn't move.* GOUNDRY *clips him over the head.*

GOUNDRY: Show the woman or I'll strip you myself.

> GOUNDRY *pulls* CORNELIUS *to his feet.*

NORA: [*to* EPSTEIN] Can't he keep his grog?

GOUNDRY: [*exploding*] You shut your mouth, you bitch.

> CORNELIUS *looks to* NORA, *both knowing that they must share a humiliation to humour this man.* CORNELIUS *lowers his trousers.* GOUNDRY *pulls up his shirt.*

What do you say, hostess?

NORA: He's man enough though still with the face... and I dare say the heart of a boy.

EPSTEIN: You've had your sport now, Goundry.

> GOUNDRY *laughs as he ruffles the boy's hair.* CORNELIUS *pulls away as he does up his trousers.* GOUNDRY *goes to exit.*

GOUNDRY: I don't have the teeth for mutton. I'll take the lamb instead.

> *He exits.*

NORA: [*to* EPSTEIN] Will you stop him?

EPSTEIN: Not when he's in this mood.

NORA: You weak bastard.

EPSTEIN: He's had nothing but the boy for months. He's out to prove
   something to himself.

NORA: Jesus...

> NORA *follows* GOUNDRY *outside.* CORNELIUS *goes to follow.*

EPSTEIN: Stay out of this.

> CORNELIUS *hesitates.*

The man is a demon and your life is worth more than the virtue of
a black girl.

◆ ◆ ◆

Outside the Rest.

NORA *follows* GOUNDRY.

NORA: Mind how you go then. For out there the blacks will see you
   before you see them.

GOUNDRY: You think I haven't handled a black before?

NORA: In a mob maybe, but not on your own. Not out there.

> GOUNDRY *hesitates.*

If it's a woman you want and a man you are, then come on. I'm
willing. I know how to please a man, Mr Goundry. And when
you're done there'll be grog on the house. [*She senses she has
him.*] Come on, the storm is nearly here and my bed is warm.

GOUNDRY: All right then... if I shut my eyes I might imagine that you're
   a whore worth having.

> *He heads back into the Rest.* NORA *casts her eye out to the
> bush, then blows out the lamp at the door before she follows
> him in.*

◆ ◆ ◆

NORA *enters the Rest.*

NORA: This way then.

> GOUNDRY *takes* CORNELIUS *by the arm and ushers him forward.*

Do you need an audience as well?

GOUNDRY: Let the boy watch. He needs to learn.

NORA: What... how to take pleasure instead of giving it?

> NORA *enters the back room.* GOUNDRY *pushes the boy after her then turns to* EPSTEIN. *He holds on him.* EPSTEIN *feels the menace behind the stillness.*

GOUNDRY: What happens on the road, Samuel, is between us. It's not for the telling. Do you understand what I'm saying to you?

> EPSTEIN *nods.*

Good. Because I don't want trouble between us. We're mates, right?

> EPSTEIN *moves away, wary.*

Are we, Samuel? Are we mates?

EPSTEIN: Yes.

GOUNDRY: I'm glad to hear it. [*Pause.*] Are you in for this then?

> *He shakes his head.*

What's the matter with you?

EPSTEIN: Nothing.

GOUNDRY: Beggars can't be choosers.

EPSTEIN: Do what you want with the woman, but I don't want any part of it.

GOUNDRY: Suit your self then.

> GOUNDRY *enters the back room.*

> *A crack of thunder as the storm breaks. The rain starts to fall like a curtain descending. Drops crack on the tin roof like balls of lead.* EPSTEIN *moves to the door and looks out. The storm builds...*

◆ ◆ ◆ ◆ ◆

SCENE TWO

Thomas Wakefield's farm—a simple bush shack.

Steady rain falling outside. WAKEFIELD *writes by the light of a lamp.*

There's a figure of a man standing outside the shack, his collar turned up against the rain. It's SAMUEL EPSTEIN. *He watches the shack for some time before he speaks.*

EPSTEIN: Mr Wakefield?

> WAKEFIELD *looks up from his writing. He takes his gun before he opens his door.*

WAKEFIELD: What do you want?

EPSTEIN: Can I step in out of the rain?

WAKEFIELD: Who are you?

EPSTEIN: Just a traveller.

WAKEFIELD: Are you alone?

EPSTEIN: I am.

> WAKEFIELD *steps back to indicate he can come inside. He keeps his gun close.* EPSTEIN *enters the shack.* WAKEFIELD *leaves the door open.*

WAKEFIELD: There's a Rest back along the road.

EPSTEIN: I know, sir. I've come from there.

WAKEFIELD: What's your business then?

EPSTEIN: The woman said you might be looking for labour.

WAKEFIELD: Did she?

EPSTEIN: There's three of us. My companions are back at the Rest. We're willing to work.

WAKEFIELD: You must be, to come asking for it on a night like this.

EPSTEIN: I've been on the road a long time. The weather doesn't bother me.

WAKEFIELD: What's your name?

EPSTEIN: Epstein. Samuel Epstein.

> *Beat.*

WAKEFIELD: Do you have a reference in your pocket from the last man you worked for, Mr Epstein?

EPSTEIN: No, I haven't.

WAKEFIELD: That's right, you haven't. Because Her Majesty doesn't write them for the likes of you, does she? [*Pause.*] What was your crime?

EPSTEIN: That's my past, sir.

WAKEFIELD: You think that's something you can leave behind?

EPSTEIN: Given a chance by a decent man, yes.

> *Beat.*

WAKEFIELD: I've got blacks to do the work.

EPSTEIN: Reliable are they?

WAKEFIELD: No. But free.

EPSTEIN: Then I'll work for free too until I've proved my worth. Then we'll discuss the other. I wouldn't want much. Just what's fair and I've heard you're a fair man, Mr Wakefield.

> *Pause.* WAKEFIELD *closes the journal he's been writing in.*

What is it you write in your book?

WAKEFIELD: My thoughts, Mr Epstein. The tasks of the day. The plans for the future... A man likes to think that one day his descendants will want to know what life out here was like.

EPSTEIN: A history?

WAKEFIELD: If you like.

EPSTEIN: I wish I could write. I'd like to think that those that come after us will know about the likes of me, as well.

> *Pause.*

WAKEFIELD: Are you any good with an axe? I've got five hundred acres of timber to clear.

EPSTEIN: I am.

WAKEFIELD: And would you stay out with the sheep? There's plenty that won't because of the blacks.

EPSTEIN: There's the three of us...

WAKEFIELD: No. One I know I can handle, but with three, you're just as likely to slit my throat.

EPSTEIN: Well... I've been on the road with them...

WAKEFIELD: That's your business. Either you want the work or you don't.

> *Pause.* WAKEFIELD *moves out onto the verandah.*

EPSTEIN: [*joining him*] I want the work enough, Mr Wakefield.

WAKEFIELD: Then show up tomorrow and we'll see.

EPSTEIN: A man in my position can't ask for more than that.

> *The night is pitch black. The rain continues to fall.*

You had any trouble from the blacks?

WAKEFIELD: There's a mob spearing sheep.

EPSTEIN: You had the need to shoot any?

WAKEFIELD: That would be murder, Epstein. I'm not a murderer.

EPSTEIN: Still, you've got the right to protect your property.

WAKEFIELD: Within the law, yes.

> *Lightning illuminates the bush. It's full of moving shadows.* WAKEFIELD *sees something out there.*

Did you see that?

EPSTEIN: What?

> *Beat. A moment of uncertainty in* WAKEFIELD.

WAKEFIELD: I thought I saw someone out there.

EPSTEIN: It's the bush, sir. She plays tricks on you at night.

> *Beat… then* WAKEFIELD *seems to dismiss it.*

WAKEFIELD: You better wait until the worst of this is over.

> *He turns and goes back inside.* EPSTEIN *looks back out into the darkness.*

❖ ❖ ❖ ❖ ❖

SCENE THREE

The Traveller's Rest.

The face of NORA *at the door staring out as the rain clears to stillness. Her hair is down. She lights the lamp at the door. She takes a bucket of water and moves outside the Rest. Everything is still and quiet.*

She lifts her long skirt and washes herself between her legs.

NORA: You might think you've had your way, Mister. But when you take a piece of Nora you get more than you bargained for. A little something that one day will make you scream in the night.

After a moment OBEDIENCE *enters the clearing. She keeps her distance from* NORA. NORA *doesn't look but she knows she's there.*

Safe then?

OBEDIENCE: [*nodding*] Them men?

NORA: Spent... for now.

NORA *holds out her steel comb.* OBEDIENCE *approaches, grateful for a reason to come to her. She starts to comb* NORA*'s hair.*

The storm has passed but we're still here. Look at it. Endless fucking plain. Soon a thousand flowers will bloom. It's a bastard to trick us like that. To make us forget what easy death lies out there.

OBEDIENCE: We could move on.

NORA: We could.

OBEDIENCE: To the sea.

NORA: Ah... the sea.

OBEDIENCE: Safe there.

NORA: You think so.

OBEDIENCE: I heard...

NORA: Here we go.

OBEDIENCE: That it's blue.

NORA: It's a lie. It's red.

OBEDIENCE *hesitates.* NORA *feels it.* OBEDIENCE *starts winding* NORA*'s hair into a bun. She brushes the girl's hand away, suddenly annoyed.*

Leave it. You're all over me.

OBEDIENCE *retreats.* CORNELIUS *watches from the door of the Rest.*

Ah... here he is, the good Mr Goundry's pupil. So did you learn anything, son? Did you learn how to touch a woman? How to run your fingers through her hair? How to stroke her cheek so that she feels something? Not bloody likely. More like the hand over the mouth to keep the screams at bay with one such as him. Am I right, boy? What, got nothing to say for yourself? Then take your sweet little face away. Your sweet little boy's face that lets him take you for a girl.

CORNELIUS *moves to strike her.*

Have you learnt that from him as well? I tell you, boy, you'll do it once and once only.

OBEDIENCE: [*trying to calm her*] Nora...

NORA: What? Have you got something to say then? Because you don't know. Thanks to me you don't know any of this.

GOUNDRY *comes out of the Rest having been woken.*

GOUNDRY: What's going on?

NORA: Nothing.

GOUNDRY: Where's Epstein?

NORA: How would I know?

ELIZABETH *enters the clearing. Her dress is drenched and stained with mud, her face and arms are cut. She stands some distance away.*

GOUNDRY: Who is she?

NORA: It's the missionary's wife...? What's happened, woman?

ELIZABETH *takes a few steps toward her then collapses to the ground.*

Get her inside.

GOUNDRY *and* CORNELIUS *take her inside and seat her by the fire.* NORA *and* OBEDIENCE *follow.*

GOUNDRY: [*to* NORA] Is it the blacks?

NORA: Out of here. Both of you. I'll deal with this.

GOUNDRY *and* CORNELIUS *move outside and away.*

Get these wet things off her.

OBEDIENCE *and* NORA *disrobe* ELIZABETH. *She wears a locket around her neck.*

The blanket.

OBEDIENCE *wraps her in a blanket.* NORA *bends down before her. She notices something about her breasts and remembers.*

Your child, woman... you're feeding a child. [*Beat.*] Where is it?

ELIZABETH: Taken.

NORA: What are you saying?

ELIZABETH: My child is taken.

NORA: And your husband?

ELIZABETH *shakes her head, unable to answer.*

[*To* OBEDIENCE] Get to Wakefield's farm, girl.

OBEDIENCE: What do I say?

NORA: Tell him what you've heard here… Tell him to get out to the mission.

OBEDIENCE *exits.*

Jesus, woman, what have you brought here?

The lights go down on this.

ACT TWO

SCENE FOUR

The Traveller's Rest.

A candle burns at the window.

A child is crying. ELIZABETH *wakes with a start. She listens rigid until the sound of the child's cry fades away. She feels the locket around her neck.*

OBEDIENCE *is sitting in the darkness watching over her.*

OBEDIENCE: There, Missus... just a dream. Night's gone away.

> ELIZABETH *settles, taking in the room around her and the white nightdress she is wearing.* NORA *enters carrying an old cloth. She blows out the candle. Dawn light at the window.*

NORA: Look... is there any place where dawn is more beautiful than this? When I see the light hit this earth, Mrs Wilkes, I want to cry... I do. An old bitch like me wants to cry.

> *Like a vivid still life, the three women are silent as the dawn light flows through the window and bathes them in its pink glow.*

Wakefield has taken a man and gone out to the mission. They'll be back by the end of the day. [*She starts to tear an old cloth into strips.*] Are you in pain... with the milk?

> ELIZABETH *nods.*

In Ireland we used the leaves of an old cabbage to bring it on... if we could spare it. But out here we just have to make do.

> *She reaches to unbutton her nightdress.* ELIZABETH *pulls away.*

Come on, woman. Modesty's a luxury you can no longer afford.

> *She relents.* NORA *unbuttons her nightdress and places the torn pieces of cloth inside her bodice. Her breasts are tender, engorged with milk.* NORA *massages them trying to bring it on.*

It's a daughter, isn't it? Your child.

> ELIZABETH *nods.*

What's her name?

ELIZABETH: Anne.

NORA: Ah... a good English name, but we won't hold that against her... It's a pretty locket you wear. What do you carry in it...? A lock of her hair?

> ELIZABETH *nods.*

Of course you do... What mother wouldn't. And her smile? Was it fair, Mrs Wilkes?

ELIZABETH: Please...

NORA: No. You must think of her. You must see her there in your arms. You must feel the warmth of her body against yours.

> ELIZABETH*'s breasts start to give milk.*

There. Now it comes... You let your breasts do the weeping.

> NORA *withdraws her hand from* ELIZABETH*'s breasts.*

It's our curse to bear the burden of our bodies. Out here there's nowhere to hide it.

> NORA *goes to leave.*

ELIZABETH: How did you know who I was?

NORA: There are not many white women this far out, Mrs Wilkes.

ELIZABETH: You knew my husband.

> *Beat.*

NORA: He came here a few times.

ELIZABETH: Why?

NORA: He would say he needed supplies. But I would say he needed the company.

> *Beat.*

ELIZABETH: I went away, you see, to have the child.

NORA: It must have been lonely for him... with you away.

ELIZABETH: He had the Lord.

NORA: I've never found the Lord much good for conversation.

> *Pause.* ELIZABETH *buttons her shirt.*

I've not borne a child, Mrs Wilkes, so I make no claim to know what it's like to lose one. Yet I regard this girl as my daughter and know how deep I hold her within me. Her skin might be black, but I've brought her up white. She's a good girl and that's no easy thing to be out here. I found her out among the saltbush, abandoned by the mother. Left for the dingoes. She's been with me ever since. She'll look after me when I'm too old to do it myself. I call her Obedience because that's what she is. Well... most of the time, isn't that right, girl?

OBEDIENCE *is silent.*

Rest now, Mrs Wilkes... it will be a long day.

◆ ◆ ◆ ◆ ◆

SCENE FIVE

A waterhole close to the Rest.

Later that morning. A bright blue sky above.

LINDA *kneels by the water. She wears a shawl draped across her shoulders. We recognise it as the one Elizabeth was holding in the opening scene. She lets it drop from her shoulders. She washes in the water, stretching her face in the palms of her hands. She hears something, a noise in the bush.*

OBEDIENCE *enters. She carries a bucket. She sees* LINDA.

Pause. OBEDIENCE *turns to go.*

LINDA: Hey...

OBEDIENCE *hesitates.*

I've seen you coming here before. Getting the water for that boss woman.

OBEDIENCE *proceeds to fill her bucket.*

You tell her to give me a job.

OBEDIENCE *doesn't answer.*

You tell her I worked for whites before. Cooking. Cleaning.

OBEDIENCE: She won't.

LINDA: Why not?

OBEDIENCE: She won't have blacks around.

> *Beat.*

LINDA: So what colour you then?

> *Beat.* OBEDIENCE *goes to move on.*

Bring me something to eat.

OBEDIENCE: She won't let me.

LINDA: I'm hungry.

OBEDIENCE: She knows what's there. [*Pause.*] You from the mission?

LINDA: [*shaking her head*] No one there anymore. All those blacks gone back to the desert.

> LINDA *wraps the shawl around her shoulders.* OBEDIENCE *starts to go, then looks back.*

OBEDIENCE: What colour's the sea?

> *Beat.*

LINDA: It's the same colour as the sky.

> *Beat.*

OBEDIENCE: I'll come later.

> OBEDIENCE *exits.*

SCENE SIX

Outside the Rest.

NORA *is washing Elizabeth's dress in a bucket.* GOUNDRY *waits nearby.* CORNELIUS *is a little way off, sharpening a stick with a knife.*

GOUNDRY: She looks frail, but she must be strong to have made her way through that storm.

NORA: The news she bore would be enough to fortify the frail.

GOUNDRY: Living among the blacks preaching God's word. What did she expect? With a babe no less. And no word of the husband.

NORA: What do you care? You're just passing through here.

GOUNDRY: Maybe we'll stay for a while. A white babe out there. It should be worth something to the men who find it... You think it was the blacks?

NORA: Pity them if it was.

GOUNDRY: Did she say as much?

NORA: She's said nothing. Been in there all day praying.

GOUNDRY: Who'd blame her for that?

NORA: You ever heard of the blacks doing such a thing?

GOUNDRY: No. But what better way to get rid of us, than to take our children... [*Beat.*] You don't know what I've seen, Nora. I know what the blacks can do. [*He indicates* CORNELIUS.] They took his parents. George and Emily Cornelius. Good people, they were. Out from Scotland to make some kind of life for themselves. She a teacher no less. I was consigned labour to them and they treated me well. But they were at them from the start, picking off their sheep one by one and burning their first crop a week before harvest. I tell you they knew what they were about. It was planned, Nora, the terror of it. But they're tough bastards, the Scots. They wouldn't be frightened off. He gives me a gun, me a convict. I could have shot his fucking head off. But he puts a gun in my hand and sends me out there to watch over his sheep. And for company he gives me his son. The mother was against it but twelve years old, he said, and old enough now to do a man's work. They were long nights, Nora, with just me and him... It was natural that something would happen between us.

NORA: Natural you say.

GOUNDRY: I know most wouldn't see it that way. But despite what you think, I have a true affection for the boy. [*Pause.*] We never saw a single black man, but sure enough if we counted twenty sheep that night there would be nineteen the next morning. Every shadow seemed to us to be of a man with his spear raised. And every sound in the bush a secret call. I'm not ashamed to tell you the terror I felt out there. We might have the guns, but what's the good of a gun if you can't see your enemy? That's what people don't get. It's a war. Them or us. And they know how to fight it... One night we see a glow in the sky. We run back to see the shack burning. The father lay outside with his gut tore open by a spear.

The mother was in the doorway with her skull bashed in. And the boy went quiet at the sight of it. Been that way ever since.

Pause.

NORA: Why are you telling me this, Goundry? I've got enough shit to carry.

She moves inside the Rest.

GOUNDRY: You're a hard bitch, Nora.

GOUNDRY *looks over at* CORNELIUS. CORNELIUS *slowly turns and meets his eye.* GOUNDRY *looks away.*

OBEDIENCE *enters the clearing carrying the bucket of water.*

There she is. Our little black princess. She wears fine clothes for a gin.

She moves toward the Rest.

Well, give her a hand. Can't you see it's heavy?

CORNELIUS *approaches to take the bucket.*

OBEDIENCE: I'm all right.

He insists. She lets him take it. He places the buckets where NORA *was washing.* OBEDIENCE *takes the dress from one bucket and starts to rinse it in another.*

GOUNDRY: What do you say, Princess? My friend here likes you. You must have seen the way he looks at you.

OBEDIENCE: I've seen.

GOUNDRY: A man shouldn't travel on his own. What do you think, would you marry him and come on the road with us?

OBEDIENCE: A woman wants a husband she can talk to.

GOUNDRY: She's a woman now, is she? Did you hear that? The haughty little bitch.

NORA *is at the door of the Rest.*

NORA: Go inside, girl. You're asking for trouble out here.

OBEDIENCE *enters the Rest.*

GOUNDRY: You cooking in there tonight?

NORA: I'll bring you something out.

GOUNDRY: What... aren't we good enough for your table now?

> NORA *takes the dress from the bucket and proceeds to hang it on a rope.*

NORA: No. You're my kind of company, Goundry. But I doubt if the missionary's wife's come across the likes of you before.

◆ ◆ ◆

Inside the Rest.

OBEDIENCE *wraps a piece of bread in a cloth.* ELIZABETH *enters from the sleeping room.*

ELIZABETH: Are they back yet?

> OBEDIENCE *shakes her head.* ELIZABETH *looks outside the Rest.*

Who are those men?

OBEDIENCE: Just travellers.

> *Beat.*

ELIZABETH: I need my dress.

OBEDIENCE: Nora's washing it.

> OBEDIENCE *goes to exit through the back, the bread wrapped in her apron.*

ELIZABETH: Obedience…

> OBEDIENCE *hesitates.*

Did you see my husband when he came here?

OBEDIENCE: Yes, Missus.

ELIZABETH: What would he do… when he was here?

OBEDIENCE: Nothing… He'd just sit and talk with Nora.

ELIZABETH: What about?

OBEDIENCE: I don't know.

ELIZABETH: You must have heard their conversations… It's all right. You can tell me.

OBEDIENCE: No, Missus… I never listened.

ELIZABETH: She's named you well, girl.

◆ ◆ ◆ ◆ ◆

SCENE SEVEN

The waterhole.

Late afternoon. Long shadows stretch across the sand.

OBEDIENCE *enters carrying a bundle.* LINDA *appears behind her.*
OBEDIENCE *turns with a start.*

LINDA: You got something then?

> OBEDIENCE *passes over the bundle.* LINDA *unwraps it and*
> *proceeds to eat.*

OBEDIENCE: She'll kill me if she finds out... Where you from?
LINDA: That mob, down by the river.
OBEDIENCE: You're the ones been taking Mr Wakefield's sheep.
LINDA: Why not? He's got plenty.

> OBEDIENCE *smiles, attracted to the defiance in the woman.* LINDA
> *continues to eat.*

OBEDIENCE: So what you doing up here? Why aren't you down at the
river with them others?

> LINDA *shrugs the question away.*

How do you know the sea is blue?
LINDA: I've seen it.
OBEDIENCE: Where?
LINDA: A long way up.
OBEDIENCE: How?
LINDA: I've been there with a white man.
OBEDIENCE: What white man?
LINDA: He's no good.
OBEDIENCE: Why?
LINDA: They're all no good.
OBEDIENCE: Why'd you go off with him then?
LINDA: [*shrugging it away*] My mother said don't look at those white
men, but I looked... Yeah, I looked. That one, he's hanging around,
looking, smiling, saying sweet things, so I went with him one night.
But the old man... my husband, he made big trouble. He said you
been with that white man now, you clear off... Ah, my mother
cried. But I didn't look back. I told all them blackfellas to bugger

off... So I went with the cattle, all over, me and him, sometimes others, but just me and him most of the time.

OBEDIENCE: Where is he?

LINDA: He found some white woman in a town up there. He told me he's marrying her now. So I told him that's all right. He can have her in his house and I'll go with him and the cattle. But he said she wouldn't like that.

OBEDIENCE: What'd you do?

LINDA: I gave him a smack across the face. Her too. I gave her such a fright she'll think twice before she looks at a black woman again.

OBEDIENCE *smiles at the thought of it.*

Yep, I had all them whites looking to give me a beating, but my bloke stopped them. He took me out to a blackfellas' camp and gave me two pounds.

OBEDIENCE: [*impressed*] Two pounds.

LINDA: That's right. You know what I did with that two pounds? I wiped my arse with it and threw it back in his face. He took me all that way from my family then leaves me with them other blackfellas. And I don't know those people, they're a different mob up there, so I wiped my arse with it and took off... Been plenty times since I wished I still had that two pounds.

OBEDIENCE: So you came back?

LINDA: What else was I going to do?

OBEDIENCE: Did they want to see you again... your mob?

LINDA: You ask a lot of questions.

Pause.

OBEDIENCE: I've seen the sea too. I don't know where. But I've seen it. And a woman's face, smiling at me... I don't know who she was, but I remember her face and I remember the sea... and it was blue. [*Going*] Stay away from the Rest. There's trouble there.

LINDA *watches her go.*

◆ ◆ ◆ ◆ ◆

SCENE EIGHT

Outside the Rest.

GOUNDRY *and* CORNELIUS *sit some distance from the Rest.* NORA *gathers wood at the wood pile.* WAKEFIELD *and* EPSTEIN *enter the clearing.* NORA *sees the look in* WAKEFIELD*'s face.*

NORA: You're a brave man, Wakefield, coming here empty-handed when there's a mother in there expecting something more.

WAKEFIELD: There's no sign of the child, just an empty crib. And the rain has done its work. There's no tracks to speak of.

NORA: And the husband?

WAKEFIELD: Let me speak to the woman.

    NORA *moves to go inside.*

Nora... the church has been burnt to the ground.

    Beat, then NORA *enters the Rest.* EPSTEIN *has joined* GOUNDRY *and* CORNELIUS.

GOUNDRY: What's going on, Samuel?

EPSTEIN: Nothing.

GOUNDRY: You take off last night and we haven't seen you till now.

EPSTEIN: I've been out to the mission with him, that's all.

GOUNDRY: How's that, then?

EPSTEIN: I was out at his place last night.

GOUNDRY: What for?

EPSTEIN: The woman said he might take us on, didn't she?

GOUNDRY: So you went by yourself.

EPSTEIN: Are you forgetting you were busy?

GOUNDRY: So did you ask?

EPSTEIN: He said he'd think about it.

GOUNDRY: Well, fuck him. If this thing works out we can forget about fence-laying for a while.

EPSTEIN: What do you mean?

GOUNDRY: Think about it. A white child out there. The men that find it will be heroes.

EPSTEIN: If it's still alive.

GOUNDRY: Alive or dead, it doesn't matter... as long as it's found.

OBEDIENCE *enters the clearing.*

EPSTEIN: I've no interest in being a hero, Goundry.

GOUNDRY: It's a chance though, isn't it?

EPSTEIN: What for?

GOUNDRY: To get a better name than the one we came here with?

> ELIZABETH *comes to the door of the Rest. She feels their eyes fall upon her.* NORA *stands behind her, blocking her impulse to retreat.* NORA *sees* OBEDIENCE.

WAKEFIELD: I'm Thomas Wakefield, Mrs Wilkes. I own property near here.

ELIZABETH: I've heard your name. My husband's mentioned it.

> *Beat.*

WAKEFIELD: Will you sit down?

ELIZABETH: No. I'll stand to hear what you've got to say.

WAKEFIELD: You've been through an ordeal.

ELIZABETH: You can't imagine what I've been through, Mr Wakefield.

> *Beat.*

WAKEFIELD: The mission is deserted. There's no sign of your child... or your husband.

ELIZABETH: I could have saved you the trip. No, there is no sign of my child for she is not there. She has been taken.

WAKEFIELD: Taken... How?

ELIZABETH: I don't know.

WAKEFIELD: Listen, Madam... we are six days ride to the nearest law. Whatever is to be done here will have to be done by ourselves. Now all I know is that this girl turned up at my house in the middle of the night to say that a child was missing. And when I got out to the mission all I found was an empty house and a burnt church. So I think now you better tell me exactly what has gone on out there.

ELIZABETH: I'll tell you and hope that you can make more sense of it than I can. [*Beat.*] I was at the waterhole... doing my washing. It's not far from the house, a few minutes walk, no more. I was in a hurry because I had left the child sleeping... besides, it was getting late, the light had begun to fade. I heard my husband approaching. He said that he had heard the child crying. So I gathered my things and started back. I found myself hurrying, almost running because I could feel it, Mr Wakefield, I could feel that something was wrong. It could have just been the storm. I could hear the thunder coming, but when I got back to the house there was nothing, no child crying, just silence. I went inside. It was dark. I reached out as any mother would, to feel for her warmth... Surely my senses played a cruel trick, for I could feel nothing there. I lit a candle, but even by the light my eyes refused the truth. The crib was empty. The child taken... I'm telling you she had fallen asleep at my breast and I had wrapped her in my shawl and put her in the crib and now she was gone. Can you understand the hell of that moment, Mr Wakefield? Can any of you imagine it...? I ran outside for my husband and saw the church burning. God help me, what was going on? I saw him running for the church. He had seen the flames and I screamed to him that the child was gone. He took his gun and told me to wait at the house until he returned. And I waited and watched our church turn to ash until I could wait no longer.

WAKEFIELD: How did the fire start? [*Beat.*] Do you think it was those who took your child?

ELIZABETH: What else can I think?

> *Beat.*

WAKEFIELD: Did your husband know the terrain out there?

ELIZABETH: He knew the area around the mission. He'd not ventured far beyond that.

WAKEFIELD: Did he take someone with him?

ELIZABETH: No.

WAKEFIELD: A tracker... someone who knew the country?

ELIZABETH: No.

WAKEFIELD: I hope for his sake he didn't go out there alone.

ELIZABETH: We had not seen the blacks for a few days. We awoke one morning and they were gone. Without forewarning or explanation.

WAKEFIELD: It was the break of the season, Mrs Wilkes. It wouldn't have occurred to them to explain what was obvious. When the rain comes food is plentiful. They have less need of the mission's supplies.

ELIZABETH: You didn't agree with our mission here, Mr Wakefield.

WAKEFIELD: I was indifferent to it.

ELIZABETH: You thought my husband was a zealot.

WAKEFIELD: I thought he misunderstood the country he had come to, that's all. The fact that he has wandered into the desert alone would prove it.

ELIZABETH: Do you think he had a choice?

WAKEFIELD: He should have come to us for help.

ELIZABETH: I have come to you for help, Mr Wakefield. Yet you seem unwilling to give it. Preferring instead to lecture me with hindsight.

> *Beat.*

WAKEFIELD: Did you see anyone at the mission that day, a stranger?

> *Pause.*

ELIZABETH: A woman had come the day before, asking for food.

WAKEFIELD: A traditional woman?

ELIZABETH: No, she wore European clothes and spoke English well enough.

WAKEFIELD: Was she a mission black?

ELIZABETH: I hadn't seen her before. I gave her bread and sent her away.

NORA: I know the one. She's been hanging around here doing the same.

> ELIZABETH's *breasts have been weeping milk. She notices the wet patches on her clothes. She feels at once exposed and ashamed.* WAKEFIELD *looks away with discretion.*

WAKEFIELD: Rest now, Mrs Wilkes, and pray that by tomorrow your child will be back in your arms.

ELIZABETH: And if my child is dead?

WAKEFIELD: Is it so easy to give up hope?

ELIZABETH: These people are nomads. What chance have we of finding her out there?

WAKEFIELD: I have seen the way they are with their children. If they have her she will be safe.

ELIZABETH: It is not their children we are talking about. But a white child, Mr Wakefield. If we lose her to the desert then she is as good as dead, for she is condemned to wander aimless and Godless. If that is to be her fate then let her meet her end now, sacrificed for some filthy rite. [*Beat.*] God's will be done.

> ELIZABETH *enters the Rest.*

NORA: Is it God's will that a child should die?

WAKEFIELD: I'll send for the law.

GOUNDRY: The law is a long way from here… Forgive me… I'm just a traveller, but a crime such as this cannot go unanswered.

WAKEFIELD: We know nothing more than the woman's story.

GOUNDRY: Do you doubt the word of a missionary's wife? [*Beat.*] If we let the blacks get away with this where will it end? I say we get a party of men together now.

WAKEFIELD: You're quick to think of vengeance, Mister.

GOUNDRY: They've burned a church. That strikes at the core of us.

WAKEFIELD: There are a dozen or more men from around here already eager to take the law into their own hands. When word of this gets out it will be hard to stop them.

GOUNDRY: Why should they be stopped?

WAKEFIELD: Let's find the woman's child first. And the husband before tomorrow's sun kills him.

> NORA *has noticed* OBEDIENCE *and can read the tension in the girl.*

NORA: What is it, girl?

> OBEDIENCE *hesitates.*

Do you know something about this?

> *She doesn't answer.*

Where have you been sneaking off to tonight?

OBEDIENCE: Nowhere.

NORA: Jesus, girl, don't you lie to me or I'll beat you black and blue.

WAKEFIELD: Obedience… you must tell us if you know something.

OBEDIENCE: It's the shawl, Mr Wakefield. She said she wrapped her baby in a shawl.

WAKEFIELD: What of it?

OBEDIENCE: I've seen the woman, the one that comes asking for food. She's wearing a shawl.

WAKEFIELD: Where is she?

> OBEDIENCE *hesitates.*

NORA: Tell him.

OBEDIENCE: The waterhole.

> OBEDIENCE *lowers her head.*

◆ ◆ ◆ ◆ ◆

SCENE NINE

Outside the Rest.

Later that night.

EPSTEIN *sits under a blanket of stars.* NORA *comes outside. She carries a bottle.*

NORA: Why didn't you go with the others?
EPSTEIN: How many men do they need to take one black woman? [*Pause.*] You think I'm a coward?
NORA: I think all men are cowards, Mr Epstein.

> *She pours them each a drink.*

EPSTEIN: Must I pay?
NORA: It's on the house. I don't much like drinking alone. And tonight I need to drink.

> *Pause.*

EPSTEIN: Do you think in England they could ever imagine a sky like this?
NORA: I don't think they give a shit what the sky is like down here. They've sent us to the end of the world, that's all they know. And it doesn't matter what kind of place we make of it. To them it will always be the end of the world. England's sewer.

> *Pause.*

EPSTEIN: [*careful*] Strange, for her not to shed a tear in the telling of such a tale.
NORA: You think you know how a woman feels?
EPSTEIN: But a mother…
NORA: Don't ask me how a mother should act. No child has passed through my cunt. It's a one-way passage. Straight to hell. Though once a man said it led him to heaven. What a night, Mr Epstein. I hovered at the pearly gates myself that night, for a while. Not for long enough mind you, but it never is long enough for a woman when a man's involved.
EPSTEIN: A man doesn't expect to find a woman like you, out here, Nora.

NORA: Not many of your kind pass this way either.

EPSTEIN: No.

NORA: How'd you get caught up with a man like Goundry?

EPSTEIN: The road's a safer place in numbers. A man offers you company, you take it.

NORA: You should be more careful in your choice of company.

EPSTEIN: I've heard some say the same to him about me.

NORA: Why... because you're foreign?

> EPSTEIN *is silent.*

We're all foreign here, aren't we?

EPSTEIN: Some of us are more foreign than others. And the blacks are the most foreign of all. Anyway, I hope to be done with Goundry soon.

NORA: How's that?

EPSTEIN: Wakefield has offered me work.

NORA: And the boy?

EPSTEIN: He won't take the three of us on.

NORA: So you'll look after yourself then?

EPSTEIN: That's right. [*Pause.*] Why do you stay out here, Nora?

NORA: Commerce. I trade on the travellers whose foolishness... or vanity, has led them to cross this continent. Halfway from where they've come, halfway to where they're going, a bowl of gruel, a mug of grog, a spot of comfort, a traveller's rest, here in this dead centre, a white island in a black sea, as far from what's civilised as I can get. [*She raises her drink to him.*] Here's to your vanity, Mr Epstein. Here's to the vanity of all men who come to tame this land—by religion, by labour, by money, by law, by their cocks, hooded or [*with a look to* EPSTEIN] cut. Yes, here's to their cocks, for there lies their weakness and my strength. Here's to them, the fools who think they're brave. [*Pouring*] Drink, drink, Mr Epstein, and pretend that you're not afraid of the night.

> *From offstage, a stifled scream.*

> *Lights reveal the sleeping room,* ELIZABETH *having woken from a dream.*

She dreams. What of? An empty crib where a child should lay? A life given, a life taken? Fear only the bitch who sheds no tears. Curse her. Curse her for her virtue and curse her for bringing it here. Drink. Let me be drunk tonight so that I don't share her dreams.

> WAKEFIELD *enters. In his hands he holds the shawl.* GOUNDRY *and* CORNELIUS *follow with* LINDA *bound at her hands and feet. She has been savagely beaten. Her clothes are torn. She is tethered by a rope held by* GOUNDRY. *He gives her no slack though clearly there's no fight left in her now.* CORNELIUS *stands with his head bowed.*

In Christ's name, Wakefield, what have you done to her?

WAKEFIELD: She fought us.

GOUNDRY: Like an animal.

WAKEFIELD: You were the animal.

GOUNDRY: I did what had to be done.

> ELIZABETH *stands rigid, hearing what's going on outside.* OBEDIENCE *comes to the door of the Rest.*

> *Through the following,* ELIZABETH *moves slowly through the Rest toward the door.*

WAKEFIELD: Tie her to the tree.

OBEDIENCE: No…

WAKEFIELD: Quiet, girl.

NORA: Go inside.

> OBEDIENCE *resists.* NORA *raises her hand to her.*

Go on.

> OBEDIENCE *flinches, then goes back into the Rest.* GOUNDRY *proceeds to chain her to the tree.*

EPSTEIN: She's not a dog.

WAKEFIELD: I have no choice.

> ELIZABETH *emerges from the Rest.* WAKEFIELD *holds out the shawl.*

Is this the cloth that wrapped your child…? Brace yourself. It's stained with blood.

> ELIZABETH *takes the cloth. She stares at it in her hands. She nods.*

And is this the woman you saw at the mission?

> ELIZABETH *hesitates, unwilling to look at* LINDA.

Look at her, Madam…

ELIZABETH *looks...*

Be certain of what you say, because a word from you will condemn her.

ELIZABETH *looks at* LINDA. *Hold.*

ELIZABETH: Yes... that's the one.

The shawl drops from her hands. She turns and goes back into the Rest.

WAKEFIELD: We'll wait for the law.

NORA: What, and keep her chained there. I'm not a jailer, Wakefield.

WAKEFIELD: If I let her go she will vanish into the desert.

EPSTEIN: Have you questioned her?

WAKEFIELD: She won't speak.

EPSTEIN: Even with the beating you've given her?

WAKEFIELD: Nothing.

EPSTEIN *approaches* LINDA.

EPSTEIN: Did you take the woman's child?

LINDA *is resolutely silent.* EPSTEIN *takes the shawl and holds it out to her.*

Listen to me... how did you come by this shawl?

LINDA *is silent.*

Speak for yourself, woman. They'll hang you for this.

LINDA *spits in his face.*

GOUNDRY: She bites the very hand that reaches out to help her.

EPSTEIN: [*wiping the spit away*] Why would she see the hand that reaches out as different to the one that strikes her? They are the same colour.

OBEDIENCE *emerges from the Rest bearing a mug of water. She walks silently through the others and stands before* LINDA, *her offering held out to her.*

Inside the Rest, during this...

ELIZABETH: [*in prayer*] On the Holy Day I went with the multitude to the house of the Lord, but his house was empty, silent and desolate. More desolate than the land. More desolate than my heart. My tears have been my meat, day and night, while others taunt me; where is thy God? Daily I reach to the depths of an empty well.

Daily I am struck by a bottomless pit. I say unto God, my rock, why hast Thou forgotten me? Bring me to the Holy Day. How long must I wait?

LINDA *raises her chained hands to* OBEDIENCE.

OBEDIENCE: I can't.

LINDA *knocks the water from her hand. She begins to wail— a sound deeply resonant to this land, but totally foreign to the European ear.*

GOUNDRY: Shut her up.

WAKEFIELD: Let her wail… she has reason enough.

GOUNDRY: There's a white child out there, man. Let me at her and I will make her talk.

WAKEFIELD: We've already beaten the woman, look at her.

GOUNDRY: She's calling her people… I've heard this before.

WAKEFIELD: We'll begin a search at sunrise.

GOUNDRY: And wait for our throats to be cut tonight?

WAKEFIELD: Shut your mouth, Goundry. Shut your fucking mouth… All of you, get out of here… go. I will speak to the woman alone.

NORA *and* OBEDIENCE *move into the Rest.*

The travellers move away into the bush.

WAKEFIELD *stands before* LINDA. *She comes to silence.*

I beg you, if the child is still alive, then pity its mother and tell us where she is and I will show you what compassion I can.

LINDA *keeps her silence.*

Your silence doesn't frighten me, woman. I've seen it too many times before. You think if you stay silent we will go away. But you don't know how far we've come and the hell we've left.

LINDA *keeps her silence.*

The lights go down on this.

◆ ◆ ◆ ◆

ACT THREE

SCENE TEN

Outside the Rest.

The next morning.

LINDA *stands chained to the tree.* OBEDIENCE *stands before her, a bowl of food in her hand. We sense she has kept this vigil for some time.* CORNELIUS *sits some distance off, watching.*

NORA *appears at the door of the Rest.*

NORA: Come in now, girl.

> OBEDIENCE *shakes her head.* NORA *watches her a moment then lets her be. She turns back into the Rest.*

OBEDIENCE: Eat something.

> LINDA *is silent.*

Please.

> LINDA *is silent.*

I had to tell them.

> LINDA *is silent.*

Did you take the Missus' baby?

> LINDA *is silent.*

They'll hang you.

> LINDA *is silent.*

I can go to your family, tell them what's happened.

> LINDA *seizes her with her eyes.*

LINDA: You… and all you other fucking whites, keep away from my family.

> *Beat.* OBEDIENCE *turns away and runs into the bush.*

◆ ◆ ◆

Inside the Rest. ELIZABETH *enters from the sleeping room. She looks out upon* LINDA.

ELIZABETH: Why won't she speak?

NORA: What would she say if she did?

> *Beat.*

ELIZABETH: Where are the men?

NORA: They left at dawn. They're searching the waterhole near the mission. [*Pause.*] Will you eat something?

> ELIZABETH *nods. She takes a place at the table.* NORA *places some food before her. She watches* ELIZABETH *as she says a silent prayer before eating.*

So devout and yet... unmoved. Where do you hide your grief?

ELIZABETH: Behind a wall of steel... How else could I bear this?

NORA: Why were you doing your washing in the evening? [*Beat.*] You said it was late and you were at the waterhole doing your washing...

> ELIZABETH *is silent.*

Most women wash in the morning then hang their clothes to dry in that day's sun.

ELIZABETH: Am I to be questioned by a whore?

NORA: You seem free enough to take her food.

ELIZABETH: You sin in the eyes of God.

NORA: Then God should turn his eyes away or, better still, pluck them out. I'm not a woman who holds much faith in religion... or law. The law is right when it suits me and wrong when it doesn't. And God? [*She spits.*] That's for God. I am beyond his condemnation. And I am beyond the condemnation of women like you.

ELIZABETH: Why do you give yourself to them?

NORA: I give nothing. They pay.

ELIZABETH: Then why do you prostitute yourself?

NORA: So that women like you can remain devout.

ELIZABETH: Like me?

NORA: Women who wear their righteousness like a pair of slender kid gloves and their precious virtue like a new summer hat? Men have a hunger, an insatiable hunger and they take as God-given their right to have their fill whenever and with whoever they please.

Why not get something for what they will take for free anyway?
Does that make me a whore in your eyes?

ELIZABETH: Does my husband and child make me holier-than-thou in
yours?

Beat.

NORA: No. I can see there's more to you than meets the eye. But in the
eyes of men you are beyond reproach. You're a missionary's wife.
They give to you without question what they'd never give to me,
a woman with neither husband nor child.

ELIZABETH: And now, if I too am a woman with neither husband nor
child? What becomes of me?

NORA: You best find yourself another husband or quickly rid yourself
of your virtue if you want to survive out here.

ELIZABETH: Did my husband come to you with that hunger?

NORA *laughs.*

Do you think it's easy for me to ask that?

NORA *quietens.*

NORA: No. Not to me.

ELIZABETH: He was a decent man. His only desire was to minister to
the spiritual needs of the natives who sought entrance to God's house.

NORA: A missionary ministers to no one's needs but his own.

Hold.

ELIZABETH: A woman with an infant, Nora, washes when she can.
Morning, noon and night if need be.

She resumes her meal.

NORA: You hide many secrets behind that wall of steel. You can open
yourself to me.

ELIZABETH: A woman who holds faith in nothing but her self, is a woman
capable of betrayal. I would be a fool to reveal myself to you.

◆ ◆ ◆ ◆ ◆

SCENE ELEVEN

The waterhole.

OBEDIENCE *runs to the waterhole. She kneels down by the water and looks at her reflection. She washes her face with the water. She senses someone. She looks up.* CORNELIUS *is watching her.*

OBEDIENCE: What do you want?

> *He puts his hands to his lips... sssh. He approaches.* OBEDIENCE *backs away. He holds up his hand to indicate that he means no harm. He opens his hand to reveal a much folded and carried piece of paper.*

What is it?

> *He unfolds it with care. It's worn at the seams and coming apart in some places. He holds it out to her.*

I don't want it.

> *He insists with silence. She relents and takes it.*

I can't read.

> *She hands it back to him but he indicates that she must keep it. He reaches out and gently touches her hair. She turns her head away.*
>
> *He reaches again and touches the side of her face. She doesn't pull away. He moves forward and kisses her.*

◆ ◆ ◆ ◆

SCENE TWELVE

The Traveller's Rest.

LINDA *stands chained to the tree.*

NORA *comes out of the Rest. It's as if she can sense the moment. She turns on* LINDA.

NORA: Where is she?

LINDA *remains silent.*

And the boy? Did you see him?

LINDA *remains silent.*

Which way did they go?

WAKEFIELD, EPSTEIN *and* GOUNDRY *enter the clearing.*

WAKEFIELD: Is she inside?

NORA *nods.* WAKEFIELD *enters the Rest.*

EPSTEIN: The husband's dead, Nora.

NORA: How?

EPSTEIN: A bullet through his head.

NORA: Jesus… when will this end?

GOUNDRY: I tell you, Wakefield doesn't have the spine to do what needs to be done here.

EPSTEIN: What's that then, Goundry?

Pause.

GOUNDRY: Where's the boy?

NORA: I've sent him for wood.

◆ ◆ ◆

WAKEFIELD *stands inside the Rest.* ELIZABETH *emerges from the sleeping room. He opens his clenched hand to reveal a gold cross.*

WAKEFIELD: We found him a mile from the mission.

She takes the cross.

ELIZABETH: And the child?

WAKEFIELD: Nothing. [*Pause.*] I have buried him there.

ELIZABETH: I want him brought here.

WAKEFIELD: Madam…

ELIZABETH: He can't lie in unconsecrated ground.

WAKEFIELD: He has been there for two days. In the full sun. Do you understand me? [*Beat.*] I have marked the place with a cross. That is consecration enough out here.

Pause.

ELIZABETH: Then it is done. Both husband and child gone.

WAKEFIELD: Your child might still be alive.

ELIZABETH: No.

WAKEFIELD: We have no body.

ELIZABETH: You said yourself, it's been two days.

WAKEFIELD: We can't be sure.

ELIZABETH: The blood on the shawl, Mr Wakefield.

WAKEFIELD: Not without a body. [*Pause.*] There is more to this that you need to know. [*Beat.*] We found your husband with his gun by his side.

She shakes her head... denying the implication.

He took his own life, Madam.

ELIZABETH: No.

WAKEFIELD: From the fall of the body...

ELIZABETH: An accident... he wasn't used to handling a gun.

WAKEFIELD: The bullet travelled through the roof of his mouth. There was no accident.

ELIZABETH: Then let his soul rot in torment.

Beat.

WAKEFIELD: He was your husband.

ELIZABETH: He was a coward. An utter coward.

Pause.

WAKEFIELD: I don't understand your lack of compassion.

ELIZABETH *turns away in anger.*

From the start you have seemed so... resolute.

ELIZABETH: Am I to be condemned for my composure? If I wept into your arms and retired to my bed would you feel more ease?

WAKEFIELD: It would be the behaviour expected from most women.

ELIZABETH: Most women do not make a life out here where gentility is a liability. I have stood by my husband's side in his desire to bring God to this country. I have needed every ounce of fortitude to do so.

WAKEFIELD: But why take his own life? What reason could there be?

ELIZABETH: There is no reason. There is no reason to any of this.

WAKEFIELD: I won't accept that.

ELIZABETH: Let it be over now.

WAKEFIELD: It can't be over until someone is brought to account.

ELIZABETH: Then bring her to account. Make her speak. Make her tell us what she has done with my child. Then bring me the body so that I can end this before it drives me mad. Because I can feel it, Mr Wakefield. I can feel it at me. I can feel it at us all.

Hold.

◆ ◆ ◆

The Traveller's Rest.

LINDA *is chained to the tree.*

WAKEFIELD *emerges from the Rest with the shawl in his hand. He stands alone for a moment gathering himself before he moves to* LINDA.

WAKEFIELD: I try to imagine the hand that spilt this blood, the instrument it held… a blunt rock? A sharp knife? I try to imagine the woman's eyes as she dug this weapon into the child's throat. I try to fathom the intent, the purpose, the madness which would bring her to shed a child's blood, but I cannot. Now tell me? Are you that woman?

LINDA *is silent.*

You need only deny it and I will free you. I make that promise to you.

LINDA: I've had a white man's promise before.

WAKEFIELD: What another white man's done has nothing to do with me. I'm giving you my word. It means more to me than you can know, woman. [*Pause.*] There's no cause here to martyr yourself.

LINDA: I won't speak… You've got no right here.

WAKEFIELD *seizes the chain and pulls her to her feet.*

WAKEFIELD: This is my right.

Hold… he casts the chain away.

Do you think this is going to stop with you?

Pause. WAKEFIELD *exits.*

LINDA *is alone, silent, vulnerable—in the face of this, all her strength gone for a moment. She is close to giving in, close to succumbing to the terror of it. There are tears pushing at the back of her eyes.*

ELIZABETH *stands at the door of the Rest, watching.* LINDA *slowly looks at her. They hold on each other until* ELIZABETH *turns away and moves back into the Rest.*

◆ ◆ ◆ ◆ ◆

SCENE THIRTEEN

The road... near the Rest.

WAKEFIELD *is returning to his farm. He holds the shawl in his hand. He sees* NORA *ahead.*

WAKEFIELD: What are you doing out here, Nora?

NORA: I'm looking for my girl. [*Pause.*] Is it true that he shot himself?

WAKEFIELD *nods.*

Do you know the reason?

WAKEFIELD: The man was filled with despair.

NORA: Despair drives me to the bottle. It does not drive me to end my own life.

WAKEFIELD: She calls him a coward.

NORA: And she's right. [*Beat.*] He had a gin, Wakefield.

WAKEFIELD: How do you know?

NORA: He's a man, isn't he?

WAKEFIELD: A man of God.

NORA: The woman had left to have the child. He was alone out there for months. He came to my table and, soaked with the piss, would cry out against her coldness. Of course he would take a gin to keep himself warm. You know yourself how easy it is.

WAKEFIELD: Be careful, Nora.

NORA: What... do you deny it? [*Pause.*] You cling to that rag like you might cling to the hem of your mother's skirt.

WAKEFIELD: I wish it was that. Then I would climb up and bury my head in her lap. I knew of no place safer.

NORA: It may have been a haven for you, but from where I come, it was an altar of death, the place she lay you as she held the pillow over your head. [*Beat.*] Do you think a mother not capable?

WAKEFIELD: Not a loving one.

NORA: Too many mouths to feed, a daughter the last born, more trouble than she's worth.

WAKEFIELD: In the bogs of Ireland, yes, when food was scarce.

NORA: A woman's mind after she has laboured can be dark. She can easily start to hate herself. A fit of melancholia, a husband's neglect or a husband too amorous before she is ready. There are a thousand reasons why, and if she hates herself then it is easy to hate what she has created. Easy to take the pillow and hold it to the child's face. Easy to take the knife and plunge it deep. Easy to leave it out among the scrub for the dingoes to steal away.

WAKEFIELD: Your insinuation is as malicious as it is far-fetched.

NORA: You are blinded by her virtue. A woman who knows what it is to give life also knows what it is to take it away. The two are not so far apart.

WAKEFIELD: This is madness.

NORA: Yes. Enter the night, man. Then you will understand the madness that makes a mother kill her child. The husband understood it well enough.

WAKEFIELD: So she finds him with a gin and kills the child for revenge?

NORA: To show him the depth of his betrayal, yes.

WAKEFIELD: In another time, Nora, you would burn at the stake for the witch you are.

NORA: Yes... and you would be the man who lights the pyre, Wakefield. I have always known the kind of man you are.

> WAKEFIELD *starts to go.*

I tell you... you have the wrong woman for this. Let her go before there's real trouble with the blacks.

WAKEFIELD: First let her deny the accusation.

> WAKEFIELD *exits.*

NORA: I want her gone, Wakefield. Before this brings us all down.

◆ ◆ ◆ ◆ ◆

SCENE FOURTEEN

The Traveller's Rest.

ELIZABETH *sits waiting, resolute.* NORA *enters.*

NORA: Has my daughter come back?
ELIZABETH: Your daughter, Nora?

      NORA *tenses, sensing the danger.*

NORA: The girl.
ELIZABETH: The one you took?

    Beat.

NORA: I found her abandoned.
ELIZABETH: It is the story you tell, but your tongue is loose whe
    you're drunk and you were often drunk with my husband.

      NORA*'s impulse is to attack but she holds herself back.*

    I understand your hatred, Nora. It is the hatred of a jealous woma
    bitter and barren, who despises any woman who makes the clai
    of mother, for she is reminded of what she can never be. And
    fill the hole she clings to the black child she stole from the arn
    of the natural mother.
NORA: Your husband was a liar.
ELIZABETH: You took the woman in and fed her grog until she could r
    longer raise her head from the dirt. And while she lay there, sic
    with her first taste of white man's spirit, you stole the child awa
NORA: She agreed that the child would be better off with me.
ELIZABETH: And is she?
NORA: She is a decent girl.
ELIZABETH: She is an outcast.
NORA: She is mine.
ELIZABETH: No. The day will come when she turns her back on yo

    Pause.

NORA: Do you know how many children I have carried? The first whe
    I was fifteen. God knows where she is. Taken from me before eve
    a look. And how many since then, ripped from my cunt befo
    they were ready. Why not take one back? You take what yc

need out here. You take and then you move on and you take from
somewhere else. That's how you survive out here. Your husband
took what he needed. You and I both know it. He hated God. I
shared that with him along with the drink. But at least I hated
from without and not from within the suffocating folds of the cloth.
I was happy to hate God. For him it was torture. Torture to be
married to you. Yes, do you hear it? He sat at my table and drank
my grog and spat out his hatred of you and your piety.

>   *Silence.*

God, woman… will nothing shake you?

ELIZABETH: We all have our place to hide, Nora. Me behind my wall
>   of steel. Him behind his cloth. And you beneath the heaving bodies
>   of passing travellers.

NORA: I'll see you undone before Wakefield for this. It won't be the
>   black woman that hangs.

>   ELIZABETH *goes into the sleeping room.*

I tell you he already suspects the mother's hand.

◆ ◆ ◆

Outside.

OBEDIENCE *enters the clearing. She stands for a moment watching* LINDA.

LINDA: What do you want from me?

OBEDIENCE: I don't know.

LINDA: You want me to like you because you've got the same skin.

OBEDIENCE: Yes.

LINDA: You want me to tell you who you are, black girl?

OBEDIENCE: Yes.

LINDA: Well, I can't.

OBEDIENCE: I want you to forgive me.

>   *Pause.*

>   NORA *comes to the door of the Rest.*

>   *Beat,* OBEDIENCE *is caught between the two women.*

NORA: Where have you been, girl?

>   OBEDIENCE *rises to face her.*

[*Approaching*] Answer me.

    OBEDIENCE *is silent.* NORA *raises her hand to slap her face.*
    OBEDIENCE *doesn't flinch.* NORA *lowers her hand.*

Once you would have cowered at the sight of my raised hand.

    OBEDIENCE *moves back toward the Rest.*

Obedience.

    OBEDIENCE *hesitates but doesn't look back.*

Are you a woman now?

    Pause... then she enters the Rest without answering.

SCENE FIFTEEN

The waterhole.

CORNELIUS, *his torso naked, kneels by the water. He washes his face,
his arms, his chest. His body glistens in the moonlight.* GOUNDRY
stands watching him from the shadows. He moves forward. CORNELIUS
senses him there. He tenses.

GOUNDRY: What's this?

    CORNELIUS *gets to his feet.*

You've got the smell of something about you, boy?

    GOUNDRY *reaches out to take the boy softly at the back of the
    neck.* CORNELIUS *pulls away.*

What? A touch of the gin has gone to your head, has it? You have
touched her, haven't you? That's for sure. You look like a boy
who now thinks he's a man.

    GOUNDRY *reaches for him, again* CORNELIUS *pulls back.*

That's what a woman's touch does, Edward... it makes us think
we're strong.

    He reaches again for him.

Don't make me hurt you. I've known you so long. And for so long
you've done the right thing by me. You've kept our secret like a

boy should. But a boy who thinks he's a man, Edward...

> GOUNDRY *takes him, with his arm around the neck, holding him firm.*

May your dead mother forgive me for this.

ACT FOUR

SCENE SEVENTEEN

The Traveller's Rest.

The next morning.

LINDA *stands chained to the tree under a fierce sun.* EPSTEIN *enters carrying the broken body of* CORNELIUS.

EPSTEIN: [*calling*] Nora.

> NORA *emerges from the Rest, followed by* OBEDIENCE.

I found him at the waterhole.

NORA: Goundry?

> EPSTEIN *nods.*

Take him inside.

> EPSTEIN *carries* CORNELIUS *inside.*

[*To* OBEDIENCE] This is your doing. I told you to stay clear of these men and their business.

> NORA *moves into the Rest.*

◆ ◆ ◆

EPSTEIN *lays* CORNELIUS *down as* NORA *enters.*

EPSTEIN: The man is a madman. He has hurt the boy before, but never like this.

NORA: He has hurt the boy every time he has touched him. Help me with him.

> *They remove his shirt to reveal bruising on his back and ribs.*

Ah, Jesus, he's broken his ribs. The bastard.

> OBEDIENCE *appears at the door.*

He'll kill him the next time. That's the only way this will end. [*To* OBEDIENCE] Bring some water.

OBEDIENCE *moves away.*

How long have you known and done nothing to stop it?

EPSTEIN: I've tried.

NORA: Well, you have not tried hard enough.

EPSTEIN: You can't talk to the man…

NORA: He needs more than talking to.

EPSTEIN: Just tend him, Nora, make him well.

NORA: I can fix his body sure enough… with time… but the boy is broken, Epstein. The boy will always be broken.

> *Pause.*

EPSTEIN: Strange bonds are formed between men on the road. [*Leaving*] I'm going out to Wakefield's…

NORA: You'll find the cause of all this trouble already there.

> EPSTEIN *exits.*

> OBEDIENCE *enters the room. She holds out the folded piece of paper she received from* CORNELIUS *the night before to* NORA.

OBEDIENCE: He gave it to me last night?

> NORA *takes the piece of paper, unfolding it with care.*

NORA: It's a letter [*She looks at* CORNELIUS.] From his mother… [*Reading*] 'My name is Emily Cornelius. A convict labourer named Nathaniel Goundry holds my son and me hostage here. He has murdered my husband and keeps us in terror. I fear he will kill me soon and take my son. I pray he is spared this fate, but should he survive then let this letter survive with him. I have told him to give it only to a person he trusts. I write this as a last gesture against fate. God help us. God help all who have come to this place. Emily Cornelius.' [*Pause.*] He killed her then?

> CORNELIUS *nods.*

And your silence?

> CORNELIUS *touches his mouth.*

He cut out your tongue?

◆ ◆ ◆ ◆ ◆

SCENE SEVENTEEN

Wakefield's farm.

WAKEFIELD *is writing. He looks up at the sound of someone approaching.* ELIZABETH *enters and stands before the shack.*

ELIZABETH: Mr Wakefield.

> *He comes out onto the verandah.*

WAKEFIELD: Has she spoken?

ELIZABETH: She keeps her silence. [*Pause.*] You've got good land here.

WAKEFIELD: It will be one day.

ELIZABETH: You've chosen the right place for your house.

WAKEFIELD: It's rough living at the moment, but maybe something more solid one day. There's good stone here.

ELIZABETH: How many acres?

WAKEFIELD: Five hundred with an offer on my neighbour's place for five hundred more.

ELIZABETH: With a thousand acres you'd be a gentleman in England.

WAKEFIELD: But then it would have been given to me and I would value it less. Here, I have worked for it. It's already in my blood... Is there something you wanted, Mrs Wilkes?

ELIZABETH: I needed to get away from the Rest. Do you blame me for that?

WAKEFIELD: No.

> *Pause.*

Will you go back? When it's over.

ELIZABETH: To England? Not if I have a choice.

WAKEFIELD: In your position, wouldn't it be best?

ELIZABETH: What would I do? Return to my parents and live as a burden to them?

WAKEFIELD: Would they take you?

ELIZABETH: Under sufferance.

WAKEFIELD: Surely, as a widow, your husband's church would offer a pension.

ELIZABETH: Save me from such a fate... a widow dependent on the

goodwill of the Church. I am not ready for that. Perhaps in my
dotage, but I am still capable of a life.
WAKEFIELD: Perhaps you'll marry again.
ELIZABETH: Perhaps.
WAKEFIELD: And have another child.
ELIZABETH: I'm not sure God would bless me in the same way twice.
Anyway, I'm beyond that age where men find widowhood
interesting.
WAKEFIELD: Is there such an age?
ELIZABETH: Oh yes, I've seen men falling over themselves in their
rush toward a young widow. Tragedy is appealing in someone
young. In her they find youth and the necessary experience with
propriety intact. It's an attractive combination. Beyond a certain
age though, tragedy in a woman is simply that. No, I won't go
back to England. Its social games are beyond me. I've better
prospects here where women are fewer in number and men less
interested in a woman's past... Don't think me callous, but a
woman needs to secure her place in the world.
WAKEFIELD: So you'll return to the colony?
ELIZABETH: Not without regrets. Despite the deprivation, like you I
find myself attached to this place.
WAKEFIELD: Even though it has cost you so much?
ELIZABETH: No. Because of it.
WAKEFIELD: There are some who doubt your story.
ELIZABETH: I know. I have felt the shift from sympathy to suspicion.
But you, do you doubt me?
WAKEFIELD: Doubt? I can't comprehend why a woman would take the
life of her own child. Yet your husband's death tells me there is
more to this than you have told.
ELIZABETH: Yes. I have kept my guard, until I have known whom to
trust.

Beat. WAKEFIELD *resists responding to her implicit invitation.*

My husband was an unhappy man.
WAKEFIELD: Nora says he had a gin.
ELIZABETH: She is wrong. There was no woman. I saw the temptation
there well enough, and if he was a different man then perhaps.
But no. There was no woman... My husband's mission was a

failure. Whilst I held firm to my faith and our purpose I watched him succumb to the desert. He thought he would lead them in from the wilderness straight to God's door. Instead they lead him into that wilderness and there he shot himself, it would seem, with little regard for me or our daughter. And of course the wife will bear the blame just as the mother will bear the blame. For she was not there by her child's side, and for that she will be held to account... no matter what the truth.

WAKEFIELD: But why? Have you asked yourself? Why would a black woman take a white child?

ELIZABETH: Ask the woman you have in custody. I am not on trial here.

WAKEFIELD: I am trying to help you.

ELIZABETH: Then believe me.

WAKEFIELD: Why?

ELIZABETH: Because I'm standing here before you, a Christian woman, and I'm telling you I did not kill my child.

Pause. EPSTEIN *enters.*

EPSTEIN: Mr Wakefield.

ELIZABETH *moves away.*

I didn't mean to disturb you.

WAKEFIELD: You've disturbed nothing.

EPSTEIN: Has Goundry been out here?

WAKEFIELD: No, why?

EPSTEIN: He took off last night. I think he means to cause trouble.

WAKEFIELD: How?

EPSTEIN: He wants to raise a party against the blacks.

WAKEFIELD: He won't find it hard. They took four sheep from me last night... If the others are taking the same loss they won't need encouragement.

EPSTEIN: Will you stop it?

WAKEFIELD: I'll be finished out here if this goes on.

EPSTEIN: Will you stop it?

WAKEFIELD: If I can.

EPSTEIN: I have to ask something of you, sir.

WAKEFIELD: What?

EPSTEIN: Does your offer of work still stand?

WAKEFIELD: Yes, when this business is over.

EPSTEIN: Then take the boy on with me, and if you won't have us both
then take him in my place.

WAKEFIELD: Why?

EPSTEIN: It's Goundry... he's hurt the boy.

WAKEFIELD: How?

EPSTEIN: He's raped him. [*Beat.*] Please, sir, I have let this boy suffer
for too long.

◆ ◆ ◆ ◆ ◆

SCENE EIGHTEEN

The Traveller's Rest.

CORNELIUS *remains on the bed.*

NORA *is scrubbing the table with a wire brush. She works feverishly,
agitated, occasionally breaking into a mumbled conversation with
herself.*

OBEDIENCE *enters from outside.* NORA *ceases her conversation but
keeps scrubbing, making a statement now for* OBEDIENCE*'s benefit.*
OBEDIENCE *senses her tension.*

OBEDIENCE: I'll do it.

NORA *throws the brush in the bucket.*

NORA: [*coming out with it*] I won't have you spending all day out there.

OBEDIENCE: I just took her some water.

NORA: There's work to do.

OBEDIENCE *takes the brush from the bucket and starts to scrub.*

Leave that.

OBEDIENCE *keeps scrubbing.*

[*Sharply*] I said leave it.

OBEDIENCE *puts the brush back.*

[*Softening, taking her hands*] Look at your hands. You'll dry
them out in that water. You've got lovely hands, soft.

She puts OBEDIENCE*'s hand to her cheek.*

You should have played the piano. I should have got you one. A bit of music in our lives. That's what we need. It's not too late. We'll get one up on the bullock dray.

OBEDIENCE: Don't, Nora.

NORA: Don't? What, what am I doing? Telling you you've got beautiful hands. Why shouldn't I say that? It's the truth. [*Beat.*] What do you say we move on, hey? We could. We've done it before.

OBEDIENCE: What about this place?

NORA: We'll find another. Something better.

OBEDIENCE: Not yet.

NORA: We'll get away from all this trouble.

OBEDIENCE: Where… where will we go?

NORA: I don't know yet.

OBEDIENCE: Back?

NORA: Back where?

OBEDIENCE: Back to where you found me.

> NORA *is stung to silence.*

Back to where my mother's from.

> *Pause.*

NORA: It's her out there, isn't it? Putting these thoughts in your head… I found you among the saltbush. She left you there.

OBEDIENCE: Maybe she was going to come back for me.

NORA: No.

OBEDIENCE: How do you know?

NORA: You've got… you've got the wrong idea there.

OBEDIENCE: She might have come back.

NORA: [*firmly*] No. [*Recovering*] You see you've got white in you. Your father… was white. You see it now, more and more, blackfellas with a touch of the chalk. They would have taken one look at you and they probably killed the woman that gave birth to you. That's what they would have done. They would have killed her and left you out in the scrub. That's how those blacks think.

OBEDIENCE: What colour's the sea? [*Beat.*] What colour is it, Nora?

NORA: It's red.

> OBEDIENCE *takes the brush from the bucket and starts to scrub the table.*

◆ ◆ ◆ ◆ ◆

SCENE NINETEEN

The Traveller's Rest.

Inside, OBEDIENCE *sits beside Cornelius's bed.*

Outside, LINDA *stands chained to the tree.* NORA *lights the lamps as night falls outside. She looks across to* LINDA *and approaches.*

NORA: If I cut these chains will you leave here? Without a word to the girl?

> LINDA *is silent.*

I'm offering your freedom, woman. Take it.

> LINDA *looks at* NORA. *She nods.* NORA *goes to the woodpile and takes the axe. She approaches* LINDA.

> GOUNDRY *enters the clearing.*

GOUNDRY: Nora...

> NORA *freezes.*

I'm hungry. I've walked twenty miles today.

> *She heads toward the Rest.*

NORA: I'll bring you something out.
GOUNDRY: I'll eat at the table tonight whether she likes it or not.
NORA: No.

> *She enters the Rest.*

GOUNDRY: You bitch... making a man eat outside like a dog.

> LINDA *has been watching.*

Take your eyes off me, woman.

> LINDA *looks away.*

Still got your mouth shut.

> *He approaches her. He grabs her mouth between his hands and turns her face toward him.*

Well, it's too late for words now. Tomorrow you'll see where this ends.

> *Inside, as* NORA *gathers some food...*

OBEDIENCE: Don't go out there, Nora.

NORA: Should he come in here instead…?

She goes outside the Rest.

Goundry… your food.

NORA *gives him a hunk of bread and a mug of tea.*

GOUNDRY: Tea? [*He throws it aside.*] Bring me a drink?

NORA: You've had enough.

GOUNDRY: There's never enough… Where's the boy?

NORA: I don't know.

GOUNDRY: Have you seen him today?

NORA: I saw him.

GOUNDRY: Was he…?

NORA: His face will not be the same again. If that's what you mean.

Pause—we see something like regret in the man.

GOUNDRY: Bring me a drink, Nora… I can't fight you for it.

NORA: What's in you, man, that makes you hate so much?

GOUNDRY: You don't know the half of it. Bring me a drink.

NORA: It's got you well and truly, hasn't it?

GOUNDRY: Please, Nora… it's a sharp edge I'm on here.

NORA: It's time for you to leave that boy alone.

GOUNDRY: Don't shame me when I'm weak.

NORA: You won't lay your hand on him again.

GOUNDRY *strikes* NORA *across the face.* LINDA *instinctively moves to take him on, the chain is the only thing holding her back.*

GOUNDRY: Come on, you black bitch. You want to take me on.

He settles, taking in what he has done to NORA. *He goes to her.*

Nora, come on, get up now.

He helps her up—she's bleeding from the mouth.

I didn't want to hurt you. I can't help myself. You've got to give me something to drink.

NORA *gets to her feet. She wipes the blood from her mouth.*

NORA: You won't touch the boy again.

GOUNDRY *raises his hand to strike her again.*

ACT FOUR

Jesus, man, you strike me again and it will be the end of you.

GOUNDRY: [*backing off*] Oh, Christ help me. [*Heading toward the Rest*] I'll get the drink myself.

NORA: You'll stay put. I'll get you your drink. But you've heard what I've said. It's over now with the boy.

Hold, then NORA *goes into the Rest.*

GOUNDRY: That boy owes me something.

Inside, NORA *takes the drink.* CORNELIUS *is at the door to the sleeping room. He has a knife in his hand.*

NORA: Get the thought of using that knife out of your head. You let me handle this.

She takes a bottle and mug and goes back outside to GOUNDRY.

GOUNDRY: He owes me.

NORA: Spare me that.

GOUNDRY *takes the bottle, ignoring the mug. He drinks as* NORA *picks up the discarded bowl and mug from earlier.*

GOUNDRY: You don't know what I've seen...

NORA: What have you seen, Goundry? You've seen no worse than me. Whatever has been done to you has been done to the rest of us, but what you have done, man... what you have done?

WAKEFIELD, EPSTEIN *and* ELIZABETH *enter the clearing.* WAKEFIELD *has his gun.*

WAKEFIELD: Goundry...

GOUNDRY: That's my name.

WAKEFIELD: You're accused of raping the boy.

GOUNDRY: [*drinking*] And who accuses me? [*Indicating* EPSTEIN] This filthy Jew. This Jew who was happy enough to be a woman to me when the desire took him.

EPSTEIN: He's lying.

GOUNDRY: Ask the man what his crime was?

Pause. WAKEFIELD *looks to* EPSTEIN. EPSTEIN *is silent.*

WAKEFIELD: Have you touched the boy as well?

EPSTEIN: No.

WAKEFIELD: Have you?

EPSTEIN: No. Though I may as well have. I never stopped him [GOUNDRY] doing so.

  Pause.

WAKEFIELD: His crime is in his past, Goundry. I've no interest in it. But you... you are beyond redemption.

GOUNDRY: You're too late, Wakefield. The word is out. It spreads as we wait. Tomorrow every white man for fifty miles will meet at the river. By dusk you'll see the water turn red.

  Hold. GOUNDRY *drinks.*

EPSTEIN: Stop it, Mr Wakefield. Don't let it happen.

WAKEFIELD: I can't unless she confesses to the crime and tells us where the child is.

EPSTEIN: She?

WAKEFIELD: Be careful, Epstein.

EPSTEIN: Of the truth?

WAKEFIELD: The black woman is the one who stands accused.

EPSTEIN: And what if her crime is no more than the theft of a shawl? My own crime was worse than that, I admit it, yet I was not hung for it, banished yes, but not hung... There's no justice in this, only vengeance.

  WAKEFIELD *approaches* LINDA.

WAKEFIELD: Do you understand what this man has said?

  LINDA *is silent.*

Tomorrow at dusk these white men will ride against your people. They want blood.

  LINDA *is silent.*

If I can go to them with your confession I can stop this.

  Pause. LINDA *feels the weight of responsibility.*

  OBEDIENCE *comes outside the Rest.* LINDA *looks to her... we see her weaken a moment.* OBEDIENCE *walks toward her.* LINDA *seems resolved to speak.*

OBEDIENCE: No...

LINDA: Listen to me...

OBEDIENCE: Don't tell.

LINDA *raises her hand to silence her.*

LINDA: I will speak… and all of you will listen… because this is what I've got to say. I took your child. I went to that mission and I took that child with its pale skin and its fair hair. I picked that sleeping baby up with its sweet face and I took her away. And I went down to the waterhole and I held that baby in my arms. And I sang her a sweet song. And she opened her eyes and looked at my face. And she smiled. She a little whitefella smiling at a black face 'cause she didn't know what the rest of you think of that face. How the rest of you hate that face. How you're scared of it. How you bash it. How you kick it. How you push it into the dirt. That baby didn't see anything in that face but the smile I was giving her right back. Then I took that baby and I walked to the water and I kissed her face then I held her under. And I felt her go tight at the cold and her little hands reaching and her eyes looking up at me through the water. And I held her there and thought of every white bastard that's walked on our country and I laughed at the lot of you.

Silence.

The sound of thunder approaching.

◆ ◆ ◆ ◆ ◆

SCENE TWENTY

The waterhole.

Later that night.

ELIZABETH *stands at the edge of the water. She holds the locket at her neck. The sound of thunder. The threat of rain. She fights with her own words.*

ELIZABETH: Do my justice, Lord, and fight my fight… fight my fight against…

There's the sound of a child crying.

Fight my fight… Do my justice, Lord. From the impure… protect me, from the deceitful protect me… protect me for I am weak… Bring me to the Holy Day…

She hears the sound of a gunshot from her memory...

No... [*She rips the locket from her neck.*] Now it is finished.

The locket falls from her hand. A lamp shines in the darkness.

EPSTEIN: [*offstage*] She's here.

WAKEFIELD *and* EPSTEIN *enter carrying lamps.*

ELIZABETH: Do you hear it...?

WAKEFIELD: What...?

ELIZABETH: The child crying.

WAKEFIELD: It's the wind, woman... Come back to the Rest...

She goes to throw herself into the water. WAKEFIELD *takes her and holds her back. In an instant she relents in his arms, taking shelter there. He holds her in an embrace.*

EPSTEIN *sees the locket on the sand and picks it up. He opens it. He takes a lock of hair and holds it in his palm.*

EPSTEIN: Is this your child's hair, Mrs Wilkes? [*He holds his palm out to* WAKEFIELD.] It's dark... the woman said the child's hair was fair.

WAKEFIELD: It's easy enough to make such a mistake.

EPSTEIN: No... she describes the white child in her imagination, not this woman's flesh and blood.

WAKEFIELD: For Christ sake, woman... is her confession a lie?

ELIZABETH *stands rigid.*

Tell me the truth.

ELIZABETH: The truth...? The truth is this, Mr Wakefield. They despised us... no... not despised, for they didn't care enough to feel that strongly. They laughed at us. They took our food and our shelter for as long as it suited them and then they left us with a half-built church. It stood there in the dust, a mocking testament to our monumental conceit. I felt their laughter... their utter indifference and I hated them for it. These people whom I had expected to love. I hated them. By the cover of night I watched them by their fires. I saw them naked and licentious, threatening all that is decent, all that is civilised. I saw a people God had chosen to ignore. I burned the church, Mr Wakefield. That is the truth. Why would the blacks bother? That's what undid my husband... their indifference. As if our presence there was some temporary irritation to be borne with good humour, until like a season with no rain it went away. And they were right. I saw him defeated by it and our bold plans come to nothing. And I hated him for it. For not standing against their indifference. For not having the will to complete the church, brick by brick, in spite of it. So I took the flame from the fire and burned it. And he answered me by putting a gun into his mouth. I put the flame to the church and watched it burn. Forgive me, Lord.

WAKEFIELD: And the child?

ELIZABETH: I went back to the house. The child was crying... but I was deaf to it. I took the gun and walked back to the waterhole. He asked me for forgiveness. And I answered him by laying the gun at his feet and walking away. I heard the shot before I'd even got back to the house... I went inside and she was gone. The crib was empty.

WAKEFIELD: You're lying, woman. For Christ sake, you are lying.

ELIZABETH *meets his eye.*

ELIZABETH: And if I'm not?

Pause.

WAKEFIELD: I'm letting her go... I will not have her blood on my hands.

He exits.

◆ ◆ ◆ ◆ ◆

SCENE TWENTY-ONE

The Traveller's Rest.

LINDA *stands chained to the tree.*

LINDA: I... want my people... I want my mother.

Slowly she takes the chain and winds it around her neck. When it is tight she falls forward. Her head hangs limp.

OBEDIENCE *comes to the Rest door. She sees* LINDA *and screams. She runs to her and struggles to free her from the chains.*

NORA *comes out of the Rest. She tries to pull* OBEDIENCE *away.*

NORA: She's dead, girl…

OBEDIENCE: [*struggling*] No…

… until NORA *forces her to stillness. She breaks from* NORA *and hugs* LINDA*'s body.*

WAKEFIELD, EPSTEIN, GOUNDRY *and finally* ELIZABETH *enter. They stand in silence before the body.*

ELIZABETH: [*quietly at first*] Our Father who art in Heaven…

OBEDIENCE: Nooo… you won't say those words for her.

ELIZABETH: Our Father who art in Heaven…

OBEDIENCE: Noooo.

ELIZABETH: These words will be said.

*Hold—*ELIZABETH*'s will silences them.*

Our Father who art in Heaven, hallow'd be Thy name. Your Kingdom come, Your will be done on earth as it is in Heaven.

The Lord's prayer builds with many voices ringing through the country…

VOICES: Forgive us our trespasses as we forgive those who trespass against us. Give us our daily bread, deliver us from evil, for Thine is the Kingdom, for ever and ever. Amen.

LINDA*'s body is lowered and carried out by the men.*

The lights go down on this.

◆ ◆ ◆ ◆ ◆

ACT FIVE

SCENE TWENTY-TWO

The next day.

NORA *is chopping wood outside the Rest. There is a sense of menace in the way she handles the axe.*

Inside, OBEDIENCE *is packing a small, battered suitcase.* CORNELIUS *struggles from the bed.*

OBEDIENCE: No.

> *He indicates that he will come with her.*

You can't come with me.

> *He takes his hand and places it on his heart.*

No...

> *He thumps his chest.*

I don't want you... you're just like all them other whitefellas. You think just because I lay with you there's something there. But there's nothing, you understand... nothing between you and me. Never can be.

> *She closes her bag and moves to the door. She hesitates for a moment but doesn't look back. She exits.*

◆ ◆ ◆

OBEDIENCE *emerges from the Rest with her suitcase in hand.* NORA *comes to stillness.*

OBEDIENCE: I don't know how to say goodbye to you.
NORA: I'll not have that word from you.
OBEDIENCE: Should I leave without saying it?
NORA: You'd steal off...

OBEDIENCE: Like a thief. [*Beat.*] Who is my mother?

NORA: She's the one that stands before you. The woman who has loved you like nothing else. A thief, yes and much worse, but the woman who has desired no more than any other woman. She is the one who took you, the product of some passing traveller's lust, and kept you by her side ever since to save you from the same fate as the woman who bore you. How many times have I stemmed the lust of a man who has desired you by offering myself in your place? Many deals have been done in my bed to keep you pure.

OBEDIENCE: Should I be grateful for that?

NORA: You owe me.

OBEDIENCE: If I had money I'd give it all to free myself from such a debt.

NORA: You ungrateful bitch.

OBEDIENCE: You say you love me.

NORA: You know I do.

OBEDIENCE: Then let me go.

NORA: She was glad to be rid of you.

OBEDIENCE: Then let her tell me.

NORA: You'll be an outcast.

OBEDIENCE: I'm an outcast here.

NORA: You're my daughter.

OBEDIENCE: No, I'm the daughter of the woman you stole me from.

> *Pause.*

NORA: We've travelled too far, you and me, since you were a babe. You'll never find her.

OBEDIENCE: I will if you tell me my name.

NORA: I won't help you to destroy me.

OBEDIENCE: Then I have a tongue and I will use it.

NORA: Go on then, get out. Go and find the slut that bore you if the grog has not done her in already. Take the face that has warmed my heart out of here, for now it makes me cold.

> *She resumes her chopping.* OBEDIENCE *takes her bag and exits unseen by* NORA.

I will not grieve the loss for long. I have lost before and will steel myself against it. [*She sees* OBEDIENCE *has gone.*] Yes, fear the bitch who sheds no tears, for she is me.

> ELIZABETH *emerges from the bush, having watched the preceding.*

ELIZABETH: So... now we have both lost a daughter, Nora.

> NORA *feels the grip on the axe tighten.*

NORA: Leave here... or I will split your skull.
ELIZABETH: Where will I go?
NORA: That's no concern of mine. I hope you rot in hell.
ELIZABETH: I am in hell, woman... I am already there.

> ELIZABETH *exits.*

> NORA *resumes her chopping.*

◆ ◆ ◆ ◆ ◆

SCENE TWENTY-THREE

Wakefield's farm.

WAKEFIELD *is driving posts in for a fence. His work is steady and deliberate. He drips with sweat.* EPSTEIN *enters, a sense of urgency about him.*

EPSTEIN: There are men gathered at the river.
WAKEFIELD: Five hundred acres to fence and five hundred more.
EPSTEIN: Mr Wakefield... don't do this.
WAKEFIELD: You want work, don't you? Then take this mallet and help me mark my land. I will pay you for an honest day's work. Take it, man, and turn your eyes away from the river, for once it's done not a word of it will be spoken.
EPSTEIN: This has nothing to do with the lost child. This is about land and the right to graze your sheep...
WAKEFIELD: We're building a nation here. It can't be done without cost.
EPSTEIN: And what kind of nation will it be?
WAKEFIELD: A proud nation one day.
EPSTEIN: You coward, Wakefield... you gutless coward. You can stuff your nation... and your job. I'll not let this happen.

EPSTEIN *exits.*

WAKEFIELD: Keep away from the river, man, for what you see there you will carry for the rest of your life.

WAKEFIELD *takes his journal from inside and comes back out onto the verandah. He rips the pages from it, letting them fall to the ground.*

ELIZABETH *enters.*

ELIZABETH: Will you take me, Mr Wakefield…? I have nowhere else to go. [*Pause.*] I… will tell you the truth.

He holds up his hand to hold her words back.

WAKEFIELD: Don't… for if you do then I can only turn you away. If you stay quiet then, yes, I can take you, for a man out here needs a woman by his side. But this is our agreement, Mrs Wilkes. You and I will be silent about what has passed. For what is not spoken will eventually fade.

ELIZABETH *steps up onto the verandah. They move inside leaving the pages of the journal on the ground.*

SCENE TWENTY-FOUR

GOUNDRY *is outside the Rest. He's drinking from a bottle.* NORA *comes outside. She can see the edge he's on.*

NORA: It will be dusk soon.

GOUNDRY: I know it.

NORA: A man should see through to the end what he has begun.

GOUNDRY: I can't find the boy… I'm lost without him.

Beat.

NORA: Finish your job at the river, Goundry, and when you are done, find my girl. Bring her back and I will give you your boy. Do what you will with him, but bring my girl to me.

Pause.

GOUNDRY *exits.* NORA *sits in silence.*
The sound of distant gunfire.

◆ ◆ ◆ ◆ ◆

SCENE TWENTY-FIVE

A rise above the river.

OBEDIENCE *stands looking down to the river plain below. She holds her battered suitcase.*

The sound of gunfire builds to the screams of people fleeing and the panic and terror of a massacre.

OBEDIENCE *turns and walks slowly to the front of the stage as the massacre proceeds, until there is silence.*

OBEDIENCE: It was dusk. The women had come in from gathering and had lit the fires. The children had been with them. They stayed down at the river to play in the last of the light. A group of older men were sitting near a large rock, talking about the activities of the day and about what would be done tomorrow. They would move on from this place soon and join a larger group for ceremony. Some of the younger men had gathered around the fires to see what the women had brought in. They were hungry and looking forward to the meal. One grandmother was angry and telling them to wait. Someone looked up and pointed. A white man was coming down the hill toward them. The women started calling the children. Two older girls ran to the river to bring them back. The old men got up and moved to meet the white man. They understood that he was afraid and was trying to warn them. They heard the shots coming from the other way. They looked to see a group of eight white men on horses crossing the river. The two girls that had gone for the children were the first to be shot. Several younger children fell quickly after. The women ran toward their children and were shot in turn. The men ran for their weapons and were cut down. One woman grabbed a small child and managed to hide her in the bush. But when she went back for another, she too was shot. When the full brunt of the shooting was over twenty-two people lay dead. Twelve of them were children. Another fourteen were injured. Eight had managed to escape in the bush. The old woman had been spared. Too old to run and too old to shoot. She sat by the fire and wept. The white men got down from their horses and shot the wounded. They made a pile of the bodies and set it alight. There was one white death. The man who had come to the camp to warn them. This is our history.

> GOUNDRY *enters from behind and watches* OBEDIENCE. *He approaches unseen by her.*

SCENE TWENTY-SIX

The Travellers Rest.

GOUNDRY *enters carrying* OBEDIENCE, *her dress ripped, her mouth bleeding, her stare vacant. He lays her on the ground.*

GOUNDRY: Nora…

> NORA *emerges from the Rest.*

I've brought back your girl. I found her on the road…

> NORA *approaches* OBEDIENCE.

They've raped her, Nora. And cut out her tongue.

NORA: Not her tongue… not her voice.

GOUNDRY: I'd say it was revenge for the raid against them.

> NORA *moves down and cradles* OBEDIENCE's *broken body.*

NORA: [*in a whisper*] What have I done?

> *She draws the girl to her.*

> CORNELIUS *appears at the door. He sees what has been done.*

There's your boy, Goundry. Take him and get out.

> CORNELIUS *moves forward. He holds a knife.*

GOUNDRY: Ah... son, don't be stupid now. Put the knife down.

> CORNELIUS *approaches, his injuries preventing easy movement. He lunges.* GOUNDRY *takes him and frees him of the knife. It drops to the ground.*

> CORNELIUS *falls.* GOUNDRY *cradles him, strokes his hair.*

I forgive you, boy. Tomorrow we'll move on... you and I.

◆ ◆ ◆ ◆ ◆

CLOSING

The Traveller's Rest.

Continued from the previous scene.

NORA *cradles* OBEDIENCE *until* OBEDIENCE *rises to her feet, determined to go on. She will not be stopped.*

NORA *rises and watches her.*

OBEDIENCE, *her body broken, her mouth bleeding, walks unsteady but determined to the edge of the clearing and looks out at the vastness before her.*

NORA *senses the moment of hesitation.*

NORA: Light the lamps, girl… Keep the night away… Let the world know we're here… As if the world cares.

    Hold.

THE END

For a full list of our titles, visit our website:

www.currency.com.au

Currency Press
The performing arts publisher
PO Box 2287
Strawberry Hills NSW 2012
Australia
enquiries@currency.com.au
Tel: (02) 9319 5877
Fax: (02) 9319 3649

ANDREW BOVELL has written extensively for theatre, film, radio and television. His stage plays include *Speaking in Tongues*, *An Ocean Out Of My Window*, *Ship of Fools*, *After Dinner* and *The Ballad of Lois Ryan*. He has collaborated on several projects including *Scenes from a Separation* (with Hannie Rayson), *Who's Afraid of the Working Class?* (with Christos Tsiolkas, Melissa Reeves, Patricia Cornelius and Irene Vela) and the feature films *Strictly Ballroom* (with Baz Luhrmann and Craig Pearce) and *Head On* (with Ana Kokkinos and Mira Robertson). *Lantana* opened in 2001 to critical acclaim.